NIGHT LIGHT

Night Light

BY

Donald Justice

REVISED EDITION

Wesleyan University Press

MIDDLETOWN, CONNECTICUT

Library of Congress Cataloging in Publication Data

Justice, Donald Rodney, 1925–
    Night light.

    I. Title.
PS3519.U825N5   1981   811'.54   81-16502
ISBN 0-8195-2106-X   AACR2
ISBN 0-8195-1106-4 (pbk.)

Manufactured in the United States of America
First printing February, 1967; *second printing July,* 1967;
third printing November 1968
Revised edition 1981

For Nat

The samovar has
Grown cold, the guitar
Wants tuning: Play, play!

Author's Note

I do not hold with those who think an author has no business going back over his work once the first bloom has worn off. For myself, I believe I can return to something very much like the original idea almost at will, provided only that enough of it had reached the page in the first place. It is in the very nature of poems, as I see it, to allow you to do just that. Most of the revisions to be found here are of recent origin, having been undertaken for a volume of selected poems; a few which appeared in that volume I have since had second thoughts about. In any case, I have felt free to rewrite, in various small ways, whatever I could, always of course with the hope of getting closer to the original idea than before.

CONTENTS

ORPHEUS OPENS HIS MORNING MAIL

Bills. Bills. From the mapmakers of hell, the repairers of fractured lutes, the bribed judges of musical contests, etc.

A note addressed to my wife, marked: *Please Forward*.

A group photograph, signed: *Your Admirers*. In their faces a certain sameness, as if "1" might, after all, be raised to some modest power; likewise in their costumes, at once transparent and identical, like those of young ladies at some debauched seminary. Already—such is my weakness—I picture the rooms into which they must once have locked themselves to read my work: those barren cells, beds ostentatiously unmade; the single pinched chrysanthemum, memorializing in a corner some withered event; the mullioned panes, high up, through which may be spied, far off, the shorn hedge behind which a pimply tomorrow crouches, exposing himself. O lassitudes!

Finally, an invitation to attend certain rites to be celebrated, come equinox, on the river bank. I am to be guest of honor. As always, I rehearse the scene in advance: the dark; the guards, tipsy as usual, sonorously snoring; a rustling, suddenly, among the reeds; the fitful illumination of ankles, whitely flashing . . . Afterwards, I shall probably be asked to recite my poems. But O my visions, my vertigoes! Have I imagined it only, the perverse gentility of their shrieks?

TIME AND WEATHER

Time and the weather wear away
The houses that our fathers built.
Their ghostly furniture remains—
All the sad sofas we have stained
With tears of boredom and of guilt,

The fraying mottoes, the stopped clocks . . .
And still sometimes these tired shapes
Haunt the damp parlors of the heart.
What Sunday prisons they recall!
And what miraculous escapes!

TO THE UNKNOWN LADY WHO WROTE THE LETTERS FOUND IN THE HATBOX

*To be sold at auction: . . . 1 brass bed, 1
walnut secretary . . . bird cages, a hatbox of
old letters . . .*
　　　　　　　　—NEWSPAPER ADVERTISEMENT

What, was there never any news?
And were your weathers always fine,
Your colds all common, and your blues
Too minor to deserve one line?

Between the lines it must have hurt
To see the neighborhood go down,
Your neighbor in his undershirt
At dusk come out to mow his lawn.

But whom to turn to to complain
Unless it might be your canaries,
And only in bird language then?
While slowly into mortuaries

The many-storied houses went
Or in deep, cataracted eyes
Displayed their signs of want—FOR RENT
And MADAM ROXIE WILL ADVISE.

THE GRANDFATHERS

Why will they never sleep?
—JOHN PEALE BISHOP

Why will they never sleep,
The old ones, the grandfathers?
Always you find them sitting
On ruined porches, deep
In the back country, at dusk,
Hawking and spitting.
They might have sat there forever,
Tapping their sticks,
Peevish, discredited gods.
Ask of the traveler how,
At road end, they will fix
You maybe with the cold
Eye of a snake or a bird
And answer not a word,
Only these blank, oracular
Headshakes or headnods.

DREAMS OF WATER

1

An odd silence
Falls as we enter
The cozy ship's-bar.

The captain, smiling,
Unfolds his spyglass
And offers to show you

The obscene shapes
Of certain islands,
Low in the offing.

I sit by in silence.

2

People in raincoats
Stand looking out from
Ends of piers.

A fog gathers;
And little tugs,
Growing uncertain

Of their position,
Start to complain
With the deep and bearded

Voices of fathers.

3

The season is ending.
White verandas
Curve away.

The hotel seems empty
But, once inside,
I hear a great splashing.

Behind doors
Grandfathers loll
In steaming tubs,

Huge, unblushing.

ODE TO A DRESSMAKER'S DUMMY

Papier-maché body; blue-and-black cotton jersey cover. Metal stand. Instructions included.
—SEARS, ROEBUCK CATALOGUE

O my coy darling, still
You wear for me the scent
Of those long afternoons we spent,
The two of us together,
Safe in the attic from the jealous eyes
Of household spies
And the remote buffooneries of the weather;
So high,
Our sole remaining neighbor was the sky,
Which, often enough, at dusk,
Leaning her cloudy shoulders on the sill,
Used to regard us with a bored and cynical eye.

How like the terrified,
Shy figure of a bride
You stood there then, without your clothes,
Drawn up into
So classic and so strict a pose
Almost, it seemed, our little attic grew
Dark with the first charmed night of the honeymoon.
Or was it only some obscure
Shape of my mother's youth I saw in you,
There where the rude shadows of the afternoon
˙Crept up your ankles and you stood
Hiding your sex as best you could?—
Prim ghost the evening light shone through.

18

MEMORY OF A PORCH

Miami, 1942

What I remember
Is how the wind chime
Commenced to stir
As she spoke of her childhood,

As though the simple
Death of a pet cat,
Buried with flowers,

Had brought to the porch
A rumor of storms
Dying out over
Some dark Atlantic.

At least I heard
The thing begin—
A thin, skeletal music—

And in the deep silence
Below all memory
The sighing of ferns
Half asleep in their boxes.

BUT THAT IS ANOTHER STORY

I do not think the ending can be right.
How can they marry and live happily
Forever, these who were so passionate
At chapter's end? Once they are settled in
The quiet country house, what will they do,
So many miles from anywhere?
Those blond ancestral ghosts crowding the stair,
Surely they disapprove? Ah me,
I fear love will catch cold and die
From pacing naked through those draftly halls
Night after night. Poor Frank! Poor Imogene!
Before them now their lives
Stretch empty as great Empire beds
After the lovers rise and the damp sheets
Are stripped by envious chambermaids.

And if the first night passes brightly enough,
What with the bonfires lit with old love letters,
That is no inexhaustible fuel, I think.
God knows how it must end, not I.
Will Frank walk out one day
Alone through the ruined orchard with his stick,
Strewing the path with lissome heads
Of buttercups? Will Imogene
Conceal in the crotches of old trees
Love notes for beardless gardeners and the like?
Meanwhile they quarrel and make it up,
Only to quarrel again. A sudden storm
Pulls the last fences down. Soon now the sheep
Will stray through the garden all night peering in
At the exhausted lovers where they sleep.

HEART

Heart, let us this once reason together.
Thou art a child no longer. Only think
What sport the neighbors have from us, not without cause.
These nightly sulks, these clamorous demonstrations!
Already they tell of thee a famous story.
An antique, balding spectacle such as thou art,
Affecting still that childish, engaging stammer
With all the seedy innocence of an overripe pomegranate!
Henceforth, let us conduct ourselves more becomingly.

And still I hear thee, beating thy little fist
Against the walls. My dear, have I not led thee,
Dawn after streaky dawn, besotted, home?
And still these threats to have off as before?
From thee, who wouldst lose thyself in the next street?
Go then, O my inseparable, this once more.
Afterwards we will take thought for our good name.

GIRL SITTING ALONE AT PARTY

You sit with hands folded—
A madonna, a rock.

And yet when your eyes move,
As they do,

As they cannot help doing,
Your eyes are dancers.

It is for them that the rooms below
Were darkened.

And when you go,
It is there, towards music.

Your shadow, though
Stays with me.

It sits with hands folded, stubbornly.
It will say nothing.

It is a dark rock
Against which the sea beats.

This is that other music, to which
I embrace your shadow.

PARTY

After midnight the charm
Begins to seem less potent,
And still the little band of initiates

Stand about in their circle
Attempting the ancient modes
Lord Bacchus himself must have invented.

If so far they have failed
To summon up any but the
Familiar demons of a banal whimsy,

Let us not imagine
That the invisible ones
Are either innocent or ignorable.

Even now as we go on
Pretending to pay them only
The politer forms of inattention,

Leer and Pinch Me and their kind
Are taking possession of
Our crowded rooms, our empty persons.

A LOCAL STORM

The first whimper of the storm
At the back door, wanting in,
Promised no such brave creature
As threatens now to perform
Black rites of the witch Nature
Publicly on our garden.

Thrice we hath circled the house
Murmuring incantations,
Doing a sort of war dance.
Does he think to frighten us
With his so primitive chants
Or merely try our patience?

The danger lies, after all,
In being led to suppose—
With Lear—that the wind dragons
Have been let loose to settle
Some private grudge of heaven's.
Still, how nice for our egos.

VARIATIONS FOR TWO PIANOS

For Thomas Higgins, pianist

There is no music now in all Arkansas.
Higgins is gone, taking both his pianos.

Movers dismantled the instruments, away
Sped the vans. The first detour untuned the strings.
There is no music now in all Arkansas.

Up Main Street, past the cold shopfronts of Conway,
The brash, self-important brick of the college,
Higgins is gone, taking both his pianos.

Warm evenings, the windows open, he would play
Something of Mozart's for his pupils, the birds.
There is no music now in all Arkansas.

How shall the mockingbird mend her trill, the jay
His eccentric attack, lacking a teacher?
Higgins is gone, taking both his pianos.

There is no music now in all Arkansas.

ANONYMOUS DRAWING

A delicate young Negro stands
With the reins of a horse clutched loosely in his hands;
So delicate, indeed, that we wonder if he can hold the spirited creature
    beside him
Until the master shall arrive to ride him.
Already the animal's nostrils widen with rage or fear.
But if we imagine him snorting, about to rear,
This boy, who should know about such things better than we,
Only stands smiling, passive and ornamental, in a fantastic livery
Of ruffles and puffed breeches,
Watching the artist, apparently, as he sketches.
Meanwhile the petty lord who must have paid
For the artist's trip up from Perugia, for the horse, for the boy, for
    everything here, in fact, has been delayed,
Kept too long by his steward, perhaps, discussing
Some business concerning the estate, or fussing
Over the details of his impeccable toilet
With a manservant whose opinion is that any alteration at all
    would spoil it.
However fast he should come hurrying now
Over this vast greensward, mopping his brow
Clear of the sweat of the fine Renaissance morning, it would be too late.
The artist will have had his revenge for being made to wait,
A revenge not only necessary but right and clever—
Simply to leave him out of the scene forever.

TO WAKEN A SMALL PERSON

You sleep at the top of streets
Up which workmen each morning
Go wheeling their bicycles

Your eyes are like the windows
Of some high attic the one
The very one you sleep in

They're shut it's raining the rain
Falls on the streets of the town
As it falls falls through your sleep

You must be dreaming these tears
Wake up please open yourself
Like a little umbrella

Hurry the sidewalks need you
The awnings not one is up
And the patient bicycles

Halted at intersections
They need you they are confused
The colors of traffic lights

Are bleeding bleeding wake up
The puddles of parking lots
Cannot contain such rainbows

AMERICAN SKETCHES

For WCW

Crossing Kansas by Train

The telephone poles
Have been holding their
Arms out
A long time now
To birds
That will not
Settle there
But pass with
Strange cawings
Westward to
Where dark trees
Gather about a
Waterhole this
Is Kansas the
Mountains start here
Just behind
The closed eyes
Of a farmer's
Sons asleep
In their workclothes

28

Poem to Be Read at 3 A.M.

Excepting the diner
On the outskirts
The town of Ladora
At 3 A.M.
Was dark but
For my headlights
And up in
One second-story room
A single light
Where someone
Was sick or
Perhaps reading
As I drove past
At seventy
Not thinking
This poem
Is for whoever
Had the light on

AFTER A PHRASE ABANDONED BY WALLACE STEVENS

The alp at the end of the street
—STEVENS' NOTEBOOKS

I

The alp at the end of the street
Occurs in the dreams of the town.
Over burgher and shopkeeper,
Massive, he broods,
A snowy-headed father
Upon those knees his children
No longer climb;
Or is reflected
In the cool, unruffled lakes of
Their minds, at evening,
After their day in the shops,
As shadow only, shapeless
As a wind that has stopped blowing.
Grandeur, it seems,
Comes down to this in the end:
A street of shops
With white shutters
Open for business . . .

2

One sits here
Like a tourist
Out of season,
Buttoned up to one's neck
Against the wind,
In the last of
The open-air cafés.

It is noon.
The burghers are leaving their shops.
Up the street,
Munching a good lunch,
They pass, nodding and bowing,
Certain of satisfaction.
There is no need
To be turning
Perpetual cartwheels.
Lords of the weather, they walk
As if upon air,
As if it sufficed,
As if the very cobbles of their lives,
Worn flat and even,
Were something to climb,
Not without difficulty.

Let us go out into the street
And greet them
As they deserve,
Leaping and dancing.

ELSEWHERES

South

The long green shutters are drawn.
Against what parades?

Closing our eyes against the sun,
We try to imagine

The darkness of an interior
Where something might still happen:

The razor lying open
On the cool marble washstand,

The drop of something—is it water?—
Upon stone floors.

North

Already it is midsummer
In the Sweden of our lives.

The peasants have joined hands,
They are circling the haystacks.

We watch from the veranda.
We sit, mufflered,

Humming the tune in snatches
Under our breath.

We tremble sometimes,
Not with emotion.

Waiting Room

Reading the signs,
We learn what to expect—

The trains late,
The machines out of order.

We learn what it is
To stare out into space.

Great farms surround us,
Squares of a checkerboard.

Taking our places, we wait,
We wait to be moved.

MEN AT FORTY

Men at forty
Learn to close softly
The doors to rooms they will not be
Coming back to.

At rest on a stair landing,
They feel it moving
Beneath them now like the deck of a ship,
Though the swell is gentle.

And deep in mirrors
They rediscover
The face of the boy as he practices tying
His father's tie there in secret

And the face of that father,
Still warm with the mystery of lather.
They are more fathers than sons themselves now.
Something is filling them, something

That is like the twilight sound
Of the crickets, immense,
Filling the woods at the foot of the slope
Behind their mortgaged houses.

EARLY POEMS

How fashionably sad those early poems are!
On their clipped lawns and hedges the snows fall.
Rains beat against the tarpaulins of their porches,
Where, Sunday mornings, the bored children sprawl,
Reading the comics before their parents rise.
—The rhymes, the meters, how they paralyze.

Who walks out through their streets tonight? No one.
You know these small towns, how all traffic stops
At ten. Idly, the street lamps gather moths,
And the pale mannequins wait inside dark shops,
Undressed, and ready for the dreams of men.
—Now the long silence. Now the beginning again.

THE THIN MAN

I indulge myself
In rich refusals.
Nothing suffices.

I hone myself to
This edge. Asleep, I
Am a horizon.

THE MISSING PERSON

He has come to report himself
A missing person.

The authorities
Hand him the forms.

He knows how they have waited
With the learned patience of barbers

In small shops, idle,
Stropping their razors.

But now that these spaces in his life
Stare up at him blankly,

Waiting to be filled in,
He does not know how to begin.

Afraid that he may not answer even
To his description of himself,

He asks for a mirror.
They reassure him

That he can be nowhere
But wherever he finds himself

From moment to moment,
Which, for the moment, is here.

And he might like to believe them.
But in the mirror

He sees what is missing.
It is himself

He sees there emerging
Slowly, as from the dark

Of a furnished room
Only by darkness,

One who receives no mail
And is known to the landlady only

For keeping himself to himself,
And for whom it will be years yet

Before he can trust to the light
This last disguise, himself.

THE MAN CLOSING UP

Improvisations on themes from Guillevic

I

Like a deserted beach,
The man closing up.

Broken glass on the rocks,
And seaweed coming in
To hang up on the rocks.

Old pilings, rotted, broken like teeth,
Where a pier was,

A mouth,
And the tide coming in.

The man closing up
Is like this.

He has no hunger
For anything,
The man closing up.

He would even try stones,
If they were offered.

But he has no hunger
For stones.

He would make his bed,
If he could sleep on it.

He would make his bed with white sheets
And disappear into the white,

Like a man diving,
If he could be certain

That the light
Would not keep him awake,

The light that reaches
To the bottom.

The man closing up
Tries the doors.

But first
He closes the windows.

And before that even
He had looked out the windows.

There was no storm coming
That he could see.

There was no one out walking
At that hour.

Still,
He closes the windows
And tries the doors.

He knows about storms
And about people

And about hours
Like that one.

There is a word for it,
A simple word,
And the word goes around.

It curves like a staircase,
And it goes up like a staircase,
And it *is* a staircase,

An iron staircase
On the side of a lighthouse.
All in his head.

And it makes no sound at all
In his head,
Unless he says it.

Then the keeper
Steps on the rung,
The bottom rung,

And the ascent beings.
Clangorous,
Rung after rung.

He wants to keep the light going,
If he can.

But the man closing up
Does not say the word.

HANDS

Les mains ne trouvaient plus
De bonheur dans les poches.
—GUILLEVIC

No longer do the hands know
The happiness of pockets.

Sometimes they hang at the sides
Like the dead weights of a clock.

Sometimes they clench into fists
Around the neck of anger.

Formerly there were brothers
To clasp, shoulders to rest on.

If now they unfold like maps,
All their countries seem foreign.

They dream of returning to
The dark home of the pockets.

They want to wash themselves clean
Of the blood of old salutes,

To scrub away the perfumes
Of the flesh they have tasted.

And all that they grasp is air.
Think of the hands as breathing,

Opening, closing. Think of
The emptiness of the hands.

47

. . .

THE EVENING OF THE MIND

Now comes the evening of the mind.
Here are the fireflies twitching in the blood;
Here is the shadow moving down the page
Where you sit reading by the garden wall.
Now the dwarf peach trees, nailed to their trellises,
Shudder and droop. You know their voices now,
Faintly the martyred peaches crying out
Your name, the name nobody knows but you.
It is the aura and the coming on.
It is the thing descending, circling, here.
And now it puts a claw out and you take it.
Thankfully in your lap you take it, so.

You said you would not go away again,
You did not want to go away—and yet,
It is as if you stood out on the dock
Watching a little boat drift out
Beyond the sawgrass shallows, the dead fish . . .
And you were in it, skimming past old snags,
Beyond, beyond, under a brazen sky
As soundless as a gong before it's struck—
Suspended how?—and now they strike it, now
The ether dream of five-years-old repeats, repeats,
And you must wake again to your own blood
And empty spaces in the throat.

THE SUICIDES

In Memory: J & G & G

If we recall your voices
As softer now, it's only
That they must have drifted back

A long way to have reached us
Here, and upon such a wind
As crosses the high passes.

Nor does the blue of your eyes
(Remembered) cast much light on
The page ripped from the tablet.

•

Once there in the labyrinth,
You were safe from your reasons.
We stand, now, at the threshold,

Peering in, but the passage,
For us, remains obscure; the
Corridors are still bloody.

•

What you meant to prove you have
Proved: we did not care for you
Nearly enough. Meanwhile the

Bay was preparing herself
To receive you, the for once
Wholly adequate female

To your dark inclinations;
Under your care the pistol
Was slowly learning to flower

In the desired explosion,
Disturbing the careful part
And the briefly recovered

Fixed smile of a forgotten
Triumph; deep within the black
Forest of childhood that tree

Was already rising which,
With the length of your body,
Would cast the double shadow.

•

The masks by which we knew you
Have been torn from you. Even
Those mirrors, to which always

You must have turned to confide,
Cannot have recognized you,
Stripped, as you were, finally.

At the end of your shadow
There sat another, waiting,
Whose back was always to us.

•

When the last door had been closed,
You watched, inwardly raging,
For the first glimpse of your selves
Approaching, jangling their keys.

Musicians of the black keys,
At last you compose yourselves.
We hear the music raging
Under the lids we have closed.

THE TOURIST FROM SYRACUSE

One of those men who can be a car salesman or
a tourist from Syracuse or a hired assassin.
—JOHN D. MACDONALD

You would not recognize me.
Mine is the face which blooms in
The dank mirrors of washrooms
As you grope for the light switch.

My eyes have the expression
Of the cold eyes of statues
Watching their pigeons return
From the feed you have scattered,

And I stand on my corner
With the same marble patience.
If I move at all, it is
At the same pace precisely

As the shade of the awning
Under which I stand waiting
And with whose blackness it seems
I am already blended.

I speak seldom, and always
In a murmur as quiet
As that of crowds which surround
The victims of accidents.

Shall I confess who I am?
My name is all names, or none.
I am the used-car salesman,
The tourist from Syracuse,

The hired assasin, waiting.
I will stand here forever
Like one who has missed his bus—
Familiar, anonymous—

On my usual corner,
The corner at which you turn
To approach that place where now
You must not hope to arrive.

BUS STOP

Lights are burning
In quiet rooms
Where lives go on
Resembling ours.

The quiet lives
That follow us—
These lives we lead
But do not own—

Stand in the rain
So quietly
When we are gone,
So quietly . . .

And the last bus
Comes letting dark
Umbrellas out—
Black flowers, black flowers.

And lives go on.
And lives go on
Like sudden lights
At street corners

Or like the lights
In quiet rooms
Left on for hours,
Burning, burning.

INCIDENT IN A ROSE GARDEN

A variation on an old theme
For MS

The gardener came running,
An old man, out of breath.
Fear had given him legs.

    Sir, I encountered Death
    Just now among the roses.
    Thin as a scythe he stood there.
    I knew him by his pictures.
    He had his black coat on,
    Black gloves, a broad black hat.
    I think he would have spoken,
    Seeing his mouth stood open.
    Big it was, with white teeth.
    As soon as he beckoned, I ran.
    I ran until I found you.
    Sir, I am quitting my job.
    I want to see my sons
    Once more before I die.
    I want to see California.

We shook hands; he was off.

And there stood Death in the garden,
Dressed like a Spanish waiter.
He had the air of someone
Who because he likes arriving
At all appointments early
Learns to think himself patient.

I watched him pinch one bloom off
And hold it to his nose—
A connoisseur of roses—
One bloom and then another.
They strewed the earth around him.
> Sir, you must be that stranger
> Who threatened my gardener.
> This is my property, sir.
> I welcome only friends here.

Death grinned, and his eyes lit up
With the pale glow of those lanterns
That workmen carry sometimes
To light their way through the dusk.
Now with great care he slid
The glove from his right hand
And held that out in greeting,
A little cage of bone.
> Sir, I knew your father,
> And we were friends at the end.
> As for your gardener,
> I did not threaten him.
> Old men mistake my gestures.
> I only meant to ask him
> To show me to his master.
> I take it you are he?

IN THE GREENROOM

For HB

How reassuring
To discover them
In the greenroom. Here,

Relaxing, they drop
The patronymics
By which we had come

To know them. The cross
Are no longer cross,
The old dance, nor have

The young sacrificed
Their advantages.
In this it is like

A kind of heaven
They rise to simply
By being themselves.

The sound of the axe
Biting the wood is
Rewound on the tape.

Nothing has happened.
What is this green for,
If not renewal?

AT A REHEARSAL OF "UNCLE VANYA"

NURSE: *The crows might get them.*

You mean well, doctor,
But are—forgive me—
A bit of a crank,

A friend they may love
But cannot listen
To long, for yawning.

When you are gone, though,
They move up close to
The stove's great belly.

Yes, they are burning
Your forests, doctor,
The dark green forests.

There is a silence
That falls between them
Like snow, like deep snow.

Horses have gone lame
Crossing the waste lands
Between two people.

We hear the old nurse
Calling her chickens
In now: *chook chook chook.*

It's cold in Russia.
We sit here, doctor
In the crows' shadow.

San Francisco, Actor's Workshop,
December, 1964

LAST DAYS OF PROSPERO

The aging magician retires to his island.
It is not so green as he remembers,
Nor does the sea caress its headlands
With the customary nuptial music.

He does not mind. He will not mind,
So long as the causeway to the island
Is not repaired, so long as the gay little
Tourist steamer never again

Lurches late into harbor, and no one
Applies for a license to reopen
The shuttered, pink casino. Better,
He thinks, an isle unvisited

Except for the sea birds come to roost
On the roofs of the thousand ruined cabañas,
Survivors, or the strayed whale, offshore,
Suspicious, surfacing to spout,

Noble as any fountain of Mílan . . .
The cave? That is as he had left it,
Amply provisioned against the days
To come. His cloak? Neat on its hanger;

The painted constellations, though faded
With damp a little, still glitter
And seem in the dark to move on course.
His books? He knows where they were drowned.

(What tempests he had caused, what lightnings
Loosed in the rigging of the world!)
If now it is all to be started up
Again, nothing lacks to his purpose.

Some change in the wording of the charm,
Some slight reshuffling of negative
And verb, perhaps—that should suffice.
And meanwhile he will pace the strand,

Debating, as old men do, with himself
Or with the waves, and still they come back at him.
Always and only with the same
Low chucklings or grand, indifferent sighs.

MEMO FROM THE DESK OF X

Re: the question of poems.
Certainly your proposal
Merits consideration.

I myself recall fondly
Old friends among the poems—
Harmless, but to what purpose?

Some few indeed we might keep
Alive, in transparent tents,
As an example to youth

Of the great waste the past was.
The white face of a poem
Turned to the wall, the almost

Visible heartbeat, the deep
But irregular breathing—
No harm to the state in this.

The average citizen
Might be the healthier for
Some such exposure. Granted.

Nevertheless, we must weigh
The cost against the result.
Aside from supervision,

Frequent transfusions of blood—
And often of some rare type—
Would have to be provided,

And guides trained to interpret
Their curious expressions
For the new generation,

Those who have had no chance to
Learn much about suffering.
We of an older order

Should be prepared to refute
All charges of nostalgia.
We must look to the future.

I am told by our experts
That an esthetic response
To straight lines and to circles

May be acquired, with study.
This strikes me as promising.
Our landscapes already are

Shifting in that direction;
Likewise our lives. This approach
Is not unrealistic.

I therefore must recommend,
Though not without some regret,
The extinction of poems.

FOR A FRESHMAN READER

After the German of Hans Magnus Enzensberger

Don't bother with odes, my son.
Timetables are more precise.

Currents are changing. Unroll
The sea charts. Watch it, don't sing.

The day will come when once more
Lists will be nailed to the door

And numbers stamped on the chest
Of anyone who says No.

Learn to be anonymous,
Learn more than I did: to change

Your identification,
Your address, your appearance.

Encyclicals make good fires,
Manifestoes are handy

For wrapping up the butter
And salt given to victims.

It will take more than anger,
It will take patience to force

The lungs of authority
With the fine deadly powder

Ground by those with the know-how,
The precisionists, like you.

TO THE HAWKS

McNamara, Rusk, Bundy

Farewell is the bell
Beginning to ring.

The children singing
Do not yet hear it.

The sun is shining
In their song. The sun

Is in fact shining
Upon the schoolyard,

On children swinging
Like tongues of a bell

Swung out on the long
Arc of a silence

That will not seem to
Have been a silence

Till it is broken,
As it is breaking.

There is a sun now
Louder than the sun

Of which the children
Are singing, brighter,

Too, than that other
Against whose brightness

Their eyes seem caught in
The act of shutting.

The young schoolteacher,
Waving one arm in

Time to the music,
Is waving farewell.

Her mouth is open
To sound the alarm.

The mouth of the world
Grows round with the sound.

February, 1965

POEM FOR A SURVIVOR

For RGS

Holding this poem
Close, like a mirror,
I breath upon it.

I watch for some sign.
There is a faint mist
Spreading across it.

It takes hold. It clings
To the lean hollows
As the sun rises,

This sun that is going
To burn the mist off.

I give you chamois
To clear the surface.

I give you this sun.

NARCISSUS AT HOME

A room composed entirely of mirrors. NARCIS-
SUS, *on a divan, a simple hand mirror
clutched to his bosom, into which he gazes lan-
guidly from time to time.*

Alone at last! But I am forgetting myself . . .

To that other—to him I imagine crouched on the far side of the glass, that
spy, condemned forever to his vain search for the promised
peephole—to him, indeed, it might appear that I was alone.

But you and I, my dear, know better.

Only you can guess what comfort it brings me to see you in there, ever
agreeable, nodding your head just as I nod mine—and which of us
greets the other first, who shall say?

And you as well. And you.

Here, if anywhere, one might be content:

To be surrounded always by what one loves best in all the world; to see,
wherever one turns, that single prospect which most allures the eye:

Like the distant view of a sea so tempting that one could imagine
drowning oneself there with pleasure:

Granted, an incomparable view.

Yet can it be possible to bear so much beauty without some taint of
suffering?

75

Even to one set apart like me, the bad days come, the times when I, like the rest, begin to doubt myself.

To have fallen in love with a simple hand mirror, amidst such a multitude at first glance so much more impressive, does that not in itself suggest that I may think of myself in rather humble terms, after all? That I may regard myself as less than handsome?

Is it conceivable?

Yes, the evidence is unmistakable: no change since the last glimpse I stole.

Never a change, never any improvement, despite this succession of tedious creams, these ointments smuggled in from the Orient, and at such cost.

If anything, a particle of deterioration. Just here, about the eyes, I should say. Yes, admittedly, a trifle wearier.

Not that I would think of blaming you, my eyes, you who have such prodigies of labor to perform, constantly peering and gazing. Will you never be still?

If, then, as it seems, I shall be obliged in the future to consider myself, in plain truth, not much above the average in appearance, that is no doubt because I am denied the privilege of seeing myself as others see me.

No longer should I be amazed when others regard me with wonder. I must learn to accustom myself to their sighs, their exclamations, those spontaneous bursts of applause which have always somewhat embarrassed me:

76

Admirers of beauty, I understand them now. There can be but the one explanation. The mirror reverses the image!

How shocked they would be if they could divine my secret, as I have theirs:

That to myself (yes, I confess it privately, only to you, my beloved, my second self) I appear rather ugly.

Yes, spectacularly ugly.

What a relief to have that said, at last.

Yes, ugly. [ECHO: *Ugly!*] Hideous. [ECHO: *Hideous!*] Grotesque. [ECHO: *Grotesque!*]

What a pleasure to hear the truth spoken, for once in my life!

And in such a voice—so like my own—how impossibly lovely!

Swoons

About the Author

DONALD JUSTICE is professor of English at the University of Iowa, and earlier taught at Syracuse University, the University of California, Irvine, Princeton University and the University of Virginia. *Night Light* is his second collection of poems, *The Summer Anniversaries*, also published by Wesleyan, his first. He won the Pulitzer Prize for Poetry in 1980 for his *Selected Poems*. His home is in Iowa City.